Umberto Saba: the Collection of Poems

Umberto Saba's Poetry Translated in English

Alessandro Baruffi

2

Copyright © 2020 by Alessandro Baruffi

All rights reserved. This book or any portion thereof may not be reproduced or used in any manner whatsoever without the express written permission of the publisher except for the use of brief quotations in a book review or scholarly journal.

First Printing: 2020

ISBN: 978-1-67812-617-9

Publisher: LiteraryJoint Press, Philadelphia, PA (USA)

www.literaryjoint.com

Ordering information for U.S. and non-U.S. trade bookstores and wholesalers: special discounts are available on quantity purchases by corporations, associations, educators, and others. For details, contact the publisher at the above listed address.

Cover: Portrait of Umberto Saba

4

A Few Words by the Translator

Today, Umberto Saba is widely recognized as one of the most prominent European poets of the 20th century. Born in the cosmopolitan port town of Trieste, under the Austro-Hungarian rule, in his youth, Saba struggled with hardship and poverty. After quitting his commercial studies, he joined the mercantile marine, and later the army, enlisting in the infantry regiment. While Saba successfully published his work for over three decades enjoying very favorable reception by critics, he remained an outsider to the Italian literary establishment. Following anti-Semitic laws and persecution, he migrated to Paris, returning to Italy only in 1943, where he remained under cover until the end of World War

II. His verses, tinged with melancholy and filled with compassion for the world's misery, are expressed in a language characterized by a sophisticated simplicity: light and rich of everyday words, yet musical and profound in poetic effect.

Table of Contents:

Trieste..11

Old Town...13

February Evening...............................15

Beginning of Summer........................17

The Goat..19

During a Military March....................21

I Loved...23

The Poet...25

Snow Blossom....................................27

Poetry...29

Children at the Soccer Stadium.......31

Thirteenth Game................................33

Goal..35

City Team..37

Three Moments..................................39

Mouth..41

To my Wife..43

Work..49

Portrait of My Little Girl.......................51

To my Daughter..................................53

My Father Has Been to Me....................55

Ulysses...57

Autumn...59

Happiness...61

My Little Girl......................................63

The Time of Ours................................65

After the Sadness...............................67

Three Streets.....................................69

I Had..73

As to Umberto Saba's Jewishness..........79

The Author..85

PIRANO. — Vista dal modo. — (Da fotografia.)

Trieste

I traversed the entire town.
Then I climbed a steep slope,
crowded at first, deserted further up,
closed by a low wall:
a nook where I sit
alone; and it seems to me that where it ends
the town ends too.

Trieste has a surly
grace. If one likes it,
it is like a rascal, harsh and voracious,
with blue eyes and hands too big
to offer a flower;
like a love
with jealousy.

Up from this slope every church, any street
I discover, whether it takes to the huddled beach,
or to the hill where, onto the rocky
top, a house, the last one, clings.
All around

circles all things
a strange air, a tormented air,
the native air.

My town that is in every of its part alive,
has a nook made just for me and my life,
pensive and reserved.

("Trieste" from "Il Canzoniere, Trieste e una donna", 1910-1912)

Old Town

Often, to go back to my house

I take an obscure alley in the old town.

Yellowy in some puddle is reflected

a lamp, and crowded is the street.

Here amongst the people that come and go

from the inn back home or to the brothel,

where are goods and men the debris

of a great sea port,

I discover, passing by, the infinite

in humility.

Here prostitute and seaman, the old man

swearing, the female quarreling,

the soldier who sits at the shop

of the fried-food lad,

the tumultuous young girl crazy

with love,

are all creatures of life

and of sufferance;

He stirs up within them, same as in me, our Lord.

Here, in the company of the humble I feel

my thought growing

purer where filthier is the way.

("Città vecchia" from "Il Canzoniere, Trieste e una donna", 1910-1912)

February Evening

February evening.

The moon rises.

In the street still it is

daylight, an evening that quickly falls.

Indifferent youngsters hugged one another;

skidding to aimless destinations.

And it is the thought

of death that, ultimately, helps to live on.

("Sera di febbraio" from "Il canzoniere, Ultime cose", 1935-1943)

16

Beginning of Summer

Sorrow, where are you? Here, I cannot see you;

every appearance is against you! The sun

gilds the city, shimmers in the sea.

All kinds of vehicles to the shore

carry around something or someone.

All is moving gladly, as if

existence were all but happiness.

("Principio d'estate" from "Il canzoniere, Ultime cose", 1935-1943)

18

The Goat

I spoke to a goat.

She was alone in the field, tethered.

Sated with grass, wet

by the rain, she was bleating.

That very bleating was fraternal

to my own sorrow. Thus answered I, at first

as a jest, then, because sorrow is eternal,

only has one voice that varies not.

Such voice was heard

lamenting in a solitary goat.

In a goat with a Semitic face

was heard complaining every other ill,

every other existence.

("La capra" from "Il Canzoniere, Casa e campagna", 1909-1910)

During a Military March

To know you as a lover and be unable to hold you,
to be far away while in my heart you blaze,
to have a tongue and be unable to talk,

to listen to this water and not bend down to drink,
to run lined-up, while with slow and late
strides I desire to pensively walk.

("Durante una marcia" from "Il Canzoniere, Versi militari", 1908)

22

I Loved

I loved worn-out words that no one

dared. I was charmed by the rhyme flower

lover,

the most ancient, difficult of all.

I loved the truth that lies in the depth,

almost a forgotten dream, which sorrow

rediscovers as a friend. Fearful, the heart

draws near, never to abandon her again.

I love you, who listens to me, and my good

card left to the end of my game.

("Amai" from "Il Canzoniere, Mediterranee," 1946)

24

The Poet

They are counted too, the poet's days,
just like for all men; but his, how varied are
they!

The hours of the day and the four seasons,
a bit less sun or less wind,
are the amusement and the company,
ever diverse, of his passions
that are always the same; and what is the
weather like
when he gets up, is the big event
of the day, his joy as soon as he awakes.
Above all he cheers up over
adverse lights, the lively sunny days
like the crowd in a long history,

where blue sky and storm are short-lived,
and they alternate messengers of misfortune and triumph.
With a rosy evening is back
his happiness, whose colours change with clouds,
if his own heart does not change.

They are counted too, the poet's days,
just like for all men; but his, how blissful are they!

("Il poeta" from "Il Canzoniere, Trieste e una donna", 1910-1912)

Snow Blossom

Up in the heavens all the angels

saw the bare fields

without leaves or flowers

and read in the children's hearts

how they love white things.

So they fluttered their wings tired of flying;

then descended lightly, lightly

the blossomed snow.

("Fior di Neve", from "Il Canzoniere", Parole, 1933-1934)

28

Poetry

It is like when to a man pounded by the wind,

blinded by snow – all around paints

the city an infernal wintry world –

along the wall, a door opens.

He enters. He finds the goodness not dead,

the sweetness of a warm nook. He lays a name

that was forgotten, a kiss on

smiley faces, which he would only portray

as obscure, in threatening dreams.

He returns

to the street, even the street is different.

The weather is fine again; the ice

is broken up by industrious hands, the light

blue

peeks back in the sky and in his heart. And he

thinks

that dire times may foretell good ones.

("Poesia" from "Il Canzoniere, Parole", 1933-1934)

Children at the Soccer Stadium

A spring rooster's
voice is that of a child; by which he records
fanciful romances and torments with a high
pitch.

By the side of the field a flag
waves solitary on a low wall.
On which, standing up and competing at each
break,
the children gave out dear names,
one by one, like arrows. It lives
within me the lovely scene; to a memory
it marries - in the evening - from my beardless
days.

Unpleasant in their haughtiness
the players passed by, right there.
They would see everything, but those little
ones.

("Fanciulli allo stadio" from "Il Canzoniere, Parole", 1933-1934)

Thirteenth Game

On the stands a small group

tried to keep warm.

And when

- boundless irradiation - the sun extinguished

behind a house its blaze, the field

made brighter the presentiment of the night.

Up and down ran the red jerseys,

the white jerseys, under a light of

strange iridescent transparency. The wind

deflected the football; the Goddess of Fortune

blinded yet again her eyes.

So pleasant

being so few, numb with cold,

united,

like the last men on a mountain,

watching from up there the last game.

("Tredicesima partita" from "Il Canzoniere, Parole", 1933-1934)

Goal

The goalkeeper fallen in the vain

last defense, against the ground hides

his face, not to see the bitter light.

His knelt teammate, urging him

with words and gesture to stand back up,

sees eyes filled with tears.

The crowd - united in its thrill - seems to brim

over

to the field. Circled the winner,

his brothers throw themselves to his neck.

Few are moments as wonderful as this,

to whom, burnt by hatred, love

is given, under the sky, to see.

By the unviolated goal the keeper

- the other one - has remained. But not his soul,

as the body found itself alone.

His joy turns into a somersault,

into kisses that he sends from afar.

Of this merriment - he says - I am part too.

("Goal" from "Il Canzoniere, Parole", 1933-1934)

City Team

Me too amongst the many I salute you, red-halberdiers,

spat

from the native land, by all the people

loved.

In trepidation I follow your game.

Unaware

you express with it ancient

marvelous things

on the green turf, in the open air, in the clear

wintry suns.

The anguishes

that whiten the hair all of a sudden

are from you so far away! The glory

gives you a fleeting

smile: the best it can offer. Hugs

from one another, merry gestures.

Young are you all, for the mother alive;

the wind carries you in her defense. He loves you

for this reason too the poet, from the others

differently - equally moved.

("Squadra paesana", from "Il Canzoniere", Parole, 1933-1934)

Three Moments

After running to the center of the turf, you offer
first your salute towards the stands.
Afterwards, what is born after,
as you turn the other side, to the one
where the crowd is darker, is not
a thing to be said, or that has a name.

The goalkeeper treads up and down like a
sentry.
The danger is far still.
Yet if in a stormy cloud it closes in, oh then
a young wild beast crouches down
and on the alert spies on.

Merriment is in the air, merriment in every

street.

If short-lived, what matters?

No offense crossed the goal line,

shouts crisscrossed like thunderbolts.

Your glory, eleven young lads,

like a river of love embellishes Trieste.

("Tre momenti" from "Il Canzoniere", Parole, 1933-1934)

Mouth

The mouth

that first offered

to my lips the rosiness of the aurora!

Still

in lovely thoughts I recall its scent.

Oh child-like mouth, dear mouth,

you spoke bold words and were

so sweet to kiss!

("Bocca" from "Il Canzoniere, Ultime cose", 1935-1943)

42

To My Wife

You are like a young,

white hen.

Her feathers ruffle

in the wind, her neck bends

down to drink, and rummages in the earth;

but, in walking, she has your slow

gait of queen,

as she proceeds on the grass

is busty and haughty.

She is better than the male.

She is like the females

of all the serene animals

who draw near to God.

Here, if my eye, if my judgment

doesn't deceive me, among these,

you find your equals,

and in no other woman.

When evening lulls

the little hens to sleep,

they make sounds that recall

those mild, sweet

voices with which you complain

about your pains, and don't know

that your voice has the soft, sad

music of the hen yards.

You are like a pregnant

heifer,

still free, and without

heaviness, merry even;

who, if someone strokes her, turns

her neck, where a tender

pink tinges her flesh.

If you meet up with her, and hear

her bellow, so mournful

is this sound that you tear

at the earth to give her

a present. In the same way,

I offer my gift to you

when you are sad.

You are like a long

bitch, that always has much

sweetness in her eyes

and ferociousness in her heart.

At your feet, she seems

a saint who burns

with an indomitable fervor

and in this way looks at you

as her God and Lord.

When at home or in the street

follows she, to anyone who tries

to approach you, her shining

white teeth uncovers.

And her love suffers

from jealousy.

You are like the fearful

rabbit. Within her narrow

cage, she stands upright

to look at you, and extends

her long, still ears;

she deprives

herself of the bran and

chicory that you bring her,

and cowers, seeking

the darkest corners.

Who might take away that food

from her? Who might take away her fur,

which she tears from herself

to add to the nest

where she will give birth?

Who would ever make you suffer?

You are like the swallow

that returns in the spring.

But each autumn will depart;

you don't have this art.

You have this of the swallow:

the light movements;

this to me, who felt and was

old, you announced another springtime.

You are like the provident

ant. The grandmother talks

about her to the child, when they

go out together in the countryside.

And thus I find you

in the bee, and in all the females

of all the serene animals

who draw near to God;

and I don't find you in any other woman.

(*"A mia moglie", from "Il Canzoniere, Casa e campagna", 1909-1910)*

Work

Once

my life was easy. The earth

gave me flowers and fruits in abundance.

Now, I plow a soil that is dry and hard.

The spade

bumps into stones, into brushwood. Delve

deep I have to, like someone searching for a

treasure.

("Lavoro" from "Il Canzoniere, Ultime cose", 1935-1943)

Portrait of My Little Girl

My little girl holding the ball in her hand,
with big eyes same colour as the sky
and the summery dress: "Daddy
- she said – today I want to go out with you".
And I thought: of the many appearances
one can admire on earth, I well know to which
can my child resemble.
Certainly, she resembles the foam, the marine foam
that whitens on the waves, and the vapor trail
that exhales from the roofs and the wind disperses;
Also she resembles the clouds, indifferent clouds
that do and undo in the clear sky;
and other light and wandering things.

("Ritratto della mia bambina" from "Il Canzoniere, Cose leggere e vaganti", 1920)

To My Daughter

My tender bud,
I love you not because on my tree
you bloomed again, but because much
weak are you and through love were you granted
to me;
oh daughter of mine, you are not the hope
of my dreams; and no more than for any
other bud is my love for you.

My life, my dear
child,
is the solitary ascent, the ascent closed
by the low wall,
where at sunset I sit
alone, facing my hidden thoughts.

While you don't reside in those thoughts up there,
in your world you make them wander;
and from near I enjoy looking again
at your conquest.

You conquer our home little by little,
and the heart of your wild mum.
As soon as you see her, your cheeks
set on fire with joy, and to her you run from the play.
In her lap such a pretty and pious
mum holds you, and delights. And her old love is oblivious.

("A mia figlia" from "Il Canzoniere, Casa e campagna", 1909-1910)

My Father Has Been to Me

"The scoundrel" my father has always been to me;
for twenty years, till I met him.
Then I saw what a kid was he,
and that this gift I have I got from him.

The same blue-eyed look carried as mine,
in bad times, was sweet and sly his smile.
Always like a pilgrim he went through the world;
more than one woman loved and nourished him.

He was cheerful and flippant; my mother
felt all the weights of life upon her.
From her fingers slipped he away like a balloon.

"Don't become – she would warn me – like you father":
and later on I well understood it on my own:
They were two breeds in age-old tenzone.

("Mio padre è stato per me" from "Il Canzoniere, Autobiografia," 1924)

Ulysses

In my youth I sailed the length

of the Dalmatian coasts. Islets

emerged from the waves' crest, where

a seabird would hung intent over prey,

covered with seaweed, slippery, pretty

like emeralds in the sun. When the high

tide and the night annihilated them, sails

scattered

downwind towards the open sea

to escape their peril. Today, my kingdom

is no man's land. The port

turns on its lights for others; as to me,

the indomitable spirit and the heart-wounding

love of life

still drive me to the wide sea.

("Ulisse" from "Il Canzoniere, Mediterranee," 1948)

Autumn

What has become of you, of your life,
my only friend, my pale wife?
Your beauty grows dolorous,
and no longer you resemble *Carmencita*.

You say: "Autumn is such a laughing season
in appearance, so much that it hurts my heart".
You say – and to a known enchantment your voice
conquers me –: "Don't you see, there in the garden,
that tree not entirely gone yet,
where every leaf that is left is a ruby?
To a woman, my friend, what a striking season
is Autumn. You know that, at its every return,

since I was a child, always have I cried".

Nothing else would you say to whom who lives at your side,

to whom who lives for you, for your own sorrow

that you hide from him; and wonders he if ever again –

soul – and wherein, and how, will you blossom again.

("Autunno" from "Il Canzoniere, Trieste e una donna", 1910-1912)

Happiness

Greedy for weights, the youth
spontaneously turns her back to the burden.
But bear it she cannot, and cries with
melancholy.

Vagrancy, evasion, poetry,
dear wonders at the later time! Later,
the air refines, and the steps grow
lighter.
Today is better than yesterday,
though happiness not yet achieved.

Someday we shall acquire the goodness
of its face, we shall see someone dissolve
like a smoke the useless sorrow.

("Felicità" from "Il Canzoniere, Parole," 1933-1934)

My Little Girl

My little girl, slender and pulpy,

is like a sapling with apples:

you eat one, another already entices you.

My dear little one is a child.

If back home late, she fears the stick,

her punishment of when she was little.

And when she does what is prohibited

she turns, and throws distrustful glances,

to see if mum is somewhere hidden.

My dear little one is too audacious.

She holds her longhaired head

in her hands, looks at me lengthily and speaks not.

"La mia fanciulla" from "Il Canzoniere, Casa e campagna, 1909-1910)

The Time of Ours

Would you know a time of the day that is prettier
than the evening? Much
prettier and less loved? It is the one
immediately preceding its sacred idleness;
the hour when intense is the work, when like a sea
the people are waving in the streets;
above the squared outlines of the houses
a faded moon, such that barely
would you discern in the deep serene.

It is the hour when you would leave the countryside
to enjoy your dear city,
from the bright gulf to the mountains,

varied in its graceful unity;

the time when my life like a swollen

river goes towards its sea;

and my thinking, the quick walking

of the people, the workmen at the top of the high

ladder, the child that as he's running jumps

onto the clanging cart, all appears

as a stopped motion, all this going

has an appearance of stillness.

It is the grand hour, the hour that best

accompanies our harvesting age.

("L'ora nostra" from "Il Canzoniere, Trieste e una donna," 1910-1912)

After the Sadness

It has the taste of a memory this bread,
eaten in this poor tavern,
where the city's port is more abandoned and
encumbered.

And I relish the beer's bitterness,
while seated, at half way back,
facing the clouded mountains and the
lighthouse.

My soul, conquered one of its own sorrow,
with new eyes in the ancient evening
looks at a pilot with his pregnant wife;
and a ship, whose old wood
glitters under the sun, with the chimney

as tall as the two masts, is a childhood
drawing, I made it's now twenty years.
And who could have foretold my life to be
so beautiful, with many sweet worries,
and much solitary glee.

("Dopo la tristezza" from "Il Canzoniere, Trieste e una donna," 1910-1912)

Three Streets

There is a street in Trieste where I see myself
mirrored in long days of closed sadness:
it is called *Via del Lazaretto Vecchio*.
Among houses like hospices, ancient, identical,
it has one note, only one, of merriment:
the sea, at the bottom of its side streets.
Perfumed with spices and tar
from warehouses with their desolate facades
the trade is in nets, cordage
for ships: one shop has a flag
for its emblem; inside, turned
towards the passer-by, women, who rarely
receive a glance, with bloodless faces bent
over the colors of all nations,
the workers serve out the sentence

that is life: innocent prisoners
gloomily stitching cheerful flags.

In Trieste, with its many sadnesses,
its beauties of sky and district,
there is an ascent called *Via del Monte*.
It begins with a synagogue
and closes with a cloister; halfway
up the street is a chapel; there from a meadow
you can discover the dark energy of life,
and the sea with its ships, the promontory,
and the crowds and the awnings of the market.
By the side of the slope is a graveyard,
abandoned, where not one funeral
enters, burials no longer take place, as long as I
can remember: the old cemetery
of the Jews, so dear to my thought,
if I think of my old ones, after so much
suffering and trading, buried there
—all alike, in spirit and appearance.

Via del Monte is the street of holy affection,

but the street of delight and love

is always Via *Domenico Rossetti.*

This green suburban district, whose colour

fades day by day, and is always

more city, less countryside, still keeps

the fascination of its best

years, its first scattered villas

and sparse rows of saplings.

Whoever walks on it in these last evenings

of summer – when every window

is open, and every one commands a far view,

where one waits, knitting, or reading –

thinks that, perhaps, his beloved

might flourish again, in the old pleasure

of living, of loving him, him only;

and to a rosy health his little son.

("Tre vie" from "Il Canzoniere, Trieste e una donna", 1910-1912)

I Had

I landed from an ignoble storm
to this hospitable house, – finally free –
I stand at the window.
I look in the sky the clouds pass by,
and the wedge of moon that whitens.

In front, *Palazzo Pitti* stands. And I ask myself
vain, ancient questions: Why, mother,
have you brought me to the world? What do I do
here, now
that I'm old, that everything else is new,
that the past is in rubbles, as I faced the uneven
trials of frightening events? The hope that death
will solve everything fades too.

I had the whole world to me; I had places
in the world where I was safe. So much light
I saw in them, that almost
I was a light myself. Remember?
You were the dearest of all my young friends,
almost a son to me, although I know not where
you might be, or if you are even alive, as at times
I think of you as a prisoner in the dreary
land in the hands of the enemy! A sense of shame
takes holds of me for that scarce food
and the provisional, hospitable roof.
The abject fascist and the greedy German
took everything away from me.

I had my own family, my own partner;
my good, wonderful *Lina*.
Alive she is, still, but now inclined to rest
more than her age would impose. And an anxious

compassion takes hold of me as I see her again,
in homes other than her own's, stoking
the fireplace with little wood. The painful
memory
of other times is heavy on my heart,
like a remorse, deep in the chest.
The abject fascist and the greedy German
took everything away from me.

I had a little girl, today she is a woman.
In her I saw the best side of myself.
Ill-fated time succeded
to take her away from me, as she sees in me
the root of her misfortune, nor her blue eyed
glance
shows the old affection for me.
The abject fascist and the greedy German
took everything away from me.

I had a beautiful city between the rocky

mountains and the bright sea. Mine,
because there was I born, especially mine,
as I discovered her as a child, and as an adult
I married her forever to Italy through poetry.
One had to live. So that
among all evils I chose the most worthy: it was the small,
rare store of antique books.
The inept fascist and the greedy German
took everything away from me.

I had a cemetry where my mother
rests, and my mother's elders. Beautiful
like a garden; and how many times with my thought
have I taken refuge in it! Obscure,
long ones exiles, grim events, they show me
that doubtful garden and that bed.
The abject fascist and the greedy German

took everything – the tombstone too – away from me.

("Avevo" from "Il Canzoniere" 1944)

As to Umberto Saba's Jewishness

SABA, UMBERTO (pseudonym of Umberto Poli; 1883–1957), Italian poet. Saba's mother, a niece of renowned Hebrew scholar Samuele David Luzzatto, was abandoned by her Catholic husband before the birth of her son, and some scholars have argued that he adopted the Hebrew surname Saba ("grandfather") as a tribute to Luzzatto; but more likely the surname was chosen by him for its assonance to his Slovenian nurse's name, Saber. In his youth, Saba struggled with hardship and poverty and, after abandoning commercial studies, joined the mercantile marine and later the army, enlisting in an infantry regiment in 1908.

His early *Versi militari* date back to those years and were later collected, with others, in *Coi miei occhi* (1912), the book which first brought him renown. Saba opened a secondhand bookshop in Trieste, his birthplace, which became a rendezvous for poets and writers. For almost thirty years he continued to publish poetry, but, despite its favorable reception by critics, he remained a literary outsider. Anti-Semitic persecution did not spare Saba: aware of the conflict between the two worlds to which he belonged, he chose to

share the fate of the Jews. He immigrated to Paris, but returned to Italy in 1943, and remained in hiding until the end of World War II. Sick and exhausted, he then returned to Trieste.

As a young man, the poet cut himself off from his mother's faith, rejecting the Jewish law by which he would have been considered Jewish. In

1911, the year of his first book of poems, he wrote a set of stories called The Jews, treating his mother's family as figures of exotic folklore. The stories are not unsympathetic, but are clearly written from a gently ironic distance. When "The Goat" gave rise to discussion, either of Saba's supposed identification with Jewish suffering or, conversely, of his supposed anti-Semitism, he protested that he had never intended such associations: "He had no conscious thought either for or against Jews. "The goat's Semitic face was just a visual device in the poem, he claimed. He identified himself as an Italian Triestine, an identity that went unchallenged until the Fascist "racial laws." And that identity spills out into the brilliant and original poems exploring the streets and squares, the small taverns and shops of Trieste, with their population of sailors, whores, derelicts, shopkeepers, and children--poems such as "Trieste," "Old Town," "Three Streets," and "The Suburb."

As was noted, "Saba is considered one of the major contemporary Italian poets. His themes include Trieste, its sailors and people, his troubled youth, his wife, daughter, and friends, human suffering, animals, and nature. His verse is tinged with melancholy and pessimism, and enriched with a deep feeling for the world's misery, and eagerness for warm human contacts. With his lucid style, and a language that is almost prosaic in its use of everyday words and expressions, Saba achieves a musical and deeply poetic effect. His works include *Il Canzoniere (1921), Autobiografia (1924), Figure e canti (1926), Tre Composizioni (1933),* and *Parole (1934).* Poems of the years 1900–54 appear in a second *Canzoniere* (1963), while a complete edition of his poems has been published in a dozen volumes.

In order to explain the inner development of his poetry, Saba wrote a detailed self-critical and autobiographical essay in *Storia e cronistoria del Canzoniere* (1948). Autobiographic details also appear in two other prose works, *Scorciatoie e raccontini (1946)* and *Ricordi-Racconti (1956)*. In the latter, some chapters collected under the title "*Gli Ebrei*" ("Jews," pp. 22–87, with a preamble by Carlo *Levi) give sketches of the life of the Jewish community of Trieste in the author's boyhood years. Among these sketches there is a description of an episode in the life of the young Luzzatto. Notes at the end of each narrative show that Saba had some knowledge of Hebrew and of the vernacular of Trieste's Jews. In his introduction to "*Gli Ebrei*" Saba emphasizes, somehow apologetically, that these tales, describing Jewish life in Trieste in an ironical and not always sympathetic way, were written at the beginning of the 20th century, far before the explosion of anti-Semitism in Europe and the tragedy of the Holocaust. Also in his poetry Saba shows ambivalence towards his Jewish roots, sometimes identifying himself with his Jewish ancestors and relatives, and sometimes criticizing them."

Credits: the Jewish Virtual Library
https://www.jewishvirtuallibrary.org/saba-umberto

The Author

Alessandro Baruffi (b. 1973) is a writer, poet, and academic researcher in the fields of American, Germanic, and Russian literature.

His published works include: "Adua Mar" (2000, Poems), "Icarus" (2006, Poems), "Jersey Blues" (2007, Poems), "24 Racconti" (2008, Short Stories), "The Poems of Trieste and Five Poems for the Game of Soccer" (2013, Translation, Umberto Saba), "Lunga è la Notte" (2015, Novel), "The Forgotten amongst the Great: a Collection of the Best Poems Translated in English" (2015, Translation, Vincenzo Cardarelli), "The Tales of Franz Kafka" (2016, Translation, Franz Kafka), "Le Poesie di Robert Frost nella Traduzione

Italiana" (2016, Translation, Robert Frost), and "Midnight 30, American Poems" (2016, Poems). "The Poems of Giovanni Pascoli (2017, Translation, Giovanni Pascoli), "Montale's Essential: The Poems of Eugenio Montale in English" (2017, Translation, Eugenio Montale), "Giuseppe Ungaretti, the Master of Hermeticism, Translated In English" (2018, Translation, Giuseppe Ungaretti), and "Gabriele D'Annunzio: The Collection of Poems in English" (2019, Translation, Gabriele D'Annunzio).

Website: **www.baruffi.me**